AF473727

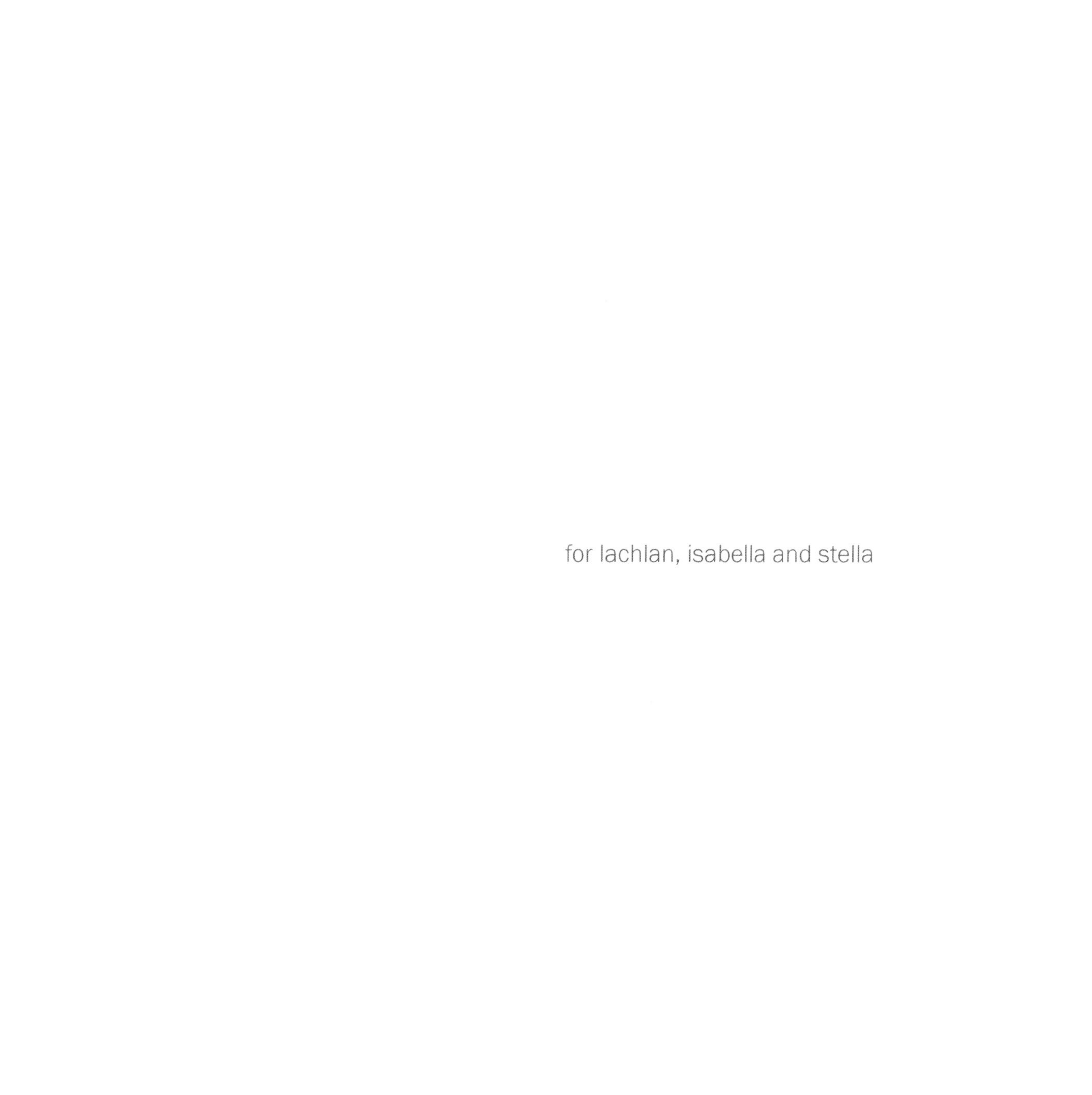

for lachlan, isabella and stella

lamp black + yellow oxide / titanium white

cadmium red transparent / may green

at first light
deer tremble
on the shore

from here you
might sail to
a lost blue

can it be
far if you
think of it

who are you
when you look
at the sea

may green / quinacridone red

blue violet / saturn red

paris blue / transparent orange

blue violet / transparent yellow

granite folds
  glaciers melt
    colour bleeds

at the edge
  where so much
    is at stake

snow lies late
  round starry
    saxifrage

cliff faces
  of sea pink
    and roseroot

sap green / perylene violet

perylene violet / phthalo green

opera rose / transparent gold green

quinacridone violet / may green

where you turn
   attention
      there is more

more and more
   bilberries
      blaeberries

given to
   be seen as
      if to say

the sheep cropped
   gentleness
      of cleared land

quinacridone gold / helio cerulean

mountain blue / opera rose brilliant

a side step
   from the path
      its pathos

sombre tones
   timbres and
      amplitudes

a depth of
   black that might
      be a time

pollen in
   the hollows
      of vowels

olive green / magenta blue violet

stay with clear
chromatic
impression

bryophytes
lichens and
sensations

which pronoun
would be best
for looking

short wild flight
small green bird
sharp wild call

ruby red / light greenish yellow

lamp black + yellow oxide / titanium white

light green / quinacridone violet

the black wood
   a remnant
      of forests

in sap green
   pine resin
      stripped spruce cone

what cannot
   be said but
      may be shown

wait a while
   some slight thing
      has withdrawn

quinacridone violet / mountain blue

scarlett red / dark olive green

graphite grey / transparent orange

birch and pine
    come in round
        about you

cold sunlight
    distributes
        harmonies

bracken fronds
    dragonflies
        impulses

pine and birch
    come in round
        about you

graphite grey / quinacridone gold orange

begin by
resembling
what you see

looking joins
a larger
enquiry

where light falls
on moss it
seems to rest

listening
learns a deep
listening

mars black / transparent sienna

olive green / magenta

transparent ochre / opera rose

as water
  trickles through
    watermint

sense flowing
  through the line
    takes its time

as water
  caresses
    watercress

the cress fresh
  currents through
    your fingers

lamp black / titanium white + neutral grey

quinacridone violet / may green + yellow transparent

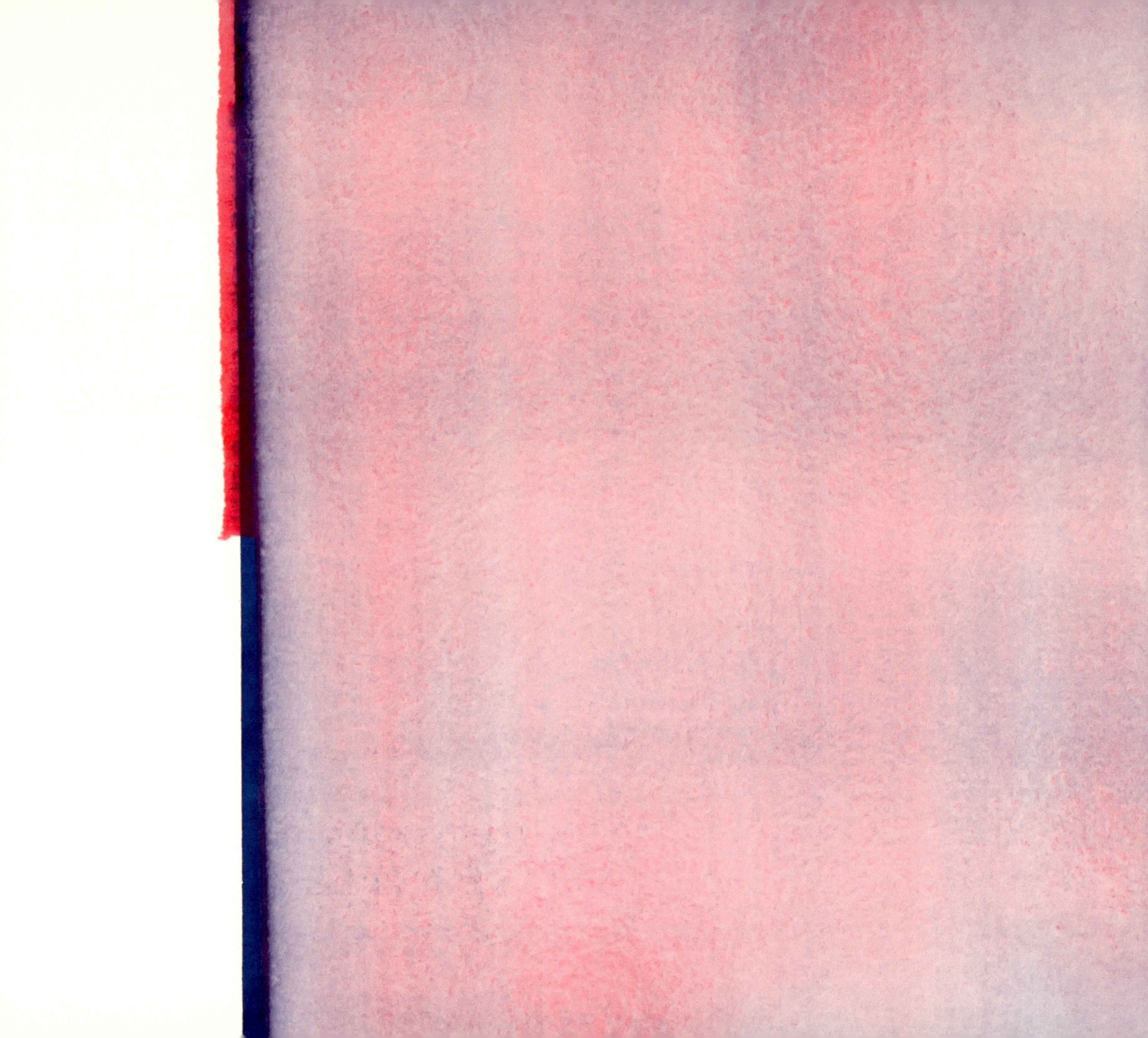

graze and browse
   blanket bog
      dwarf shrub heath

reduction
   discovers
      plenitude

what is held
   in common
      the pure land

from scorched earth
   primroses
      celandines

anthracite lamp black / titanium white

anthracite lamp black / transparent orange

mars black / transparent sienna

mars black + olive green / transparent sienna

in dark times
   the colours
      shine and sing

charcoal grey
   sapphire blue
      madder lake

you gather
   the glimmers
      the gleanings

you amber
   you umber
      you ember

olive green dark / transparent sienna

permanent rose / olive green + yellow transparent

the dusk task
  is to feel
    out into

bog cotton
  snagged wool
    dusk and smoke

what finds you
  what moves you
    what leaves you

still some light
  on the pool
    in the wood

olive green + transparent yellow / ruby red

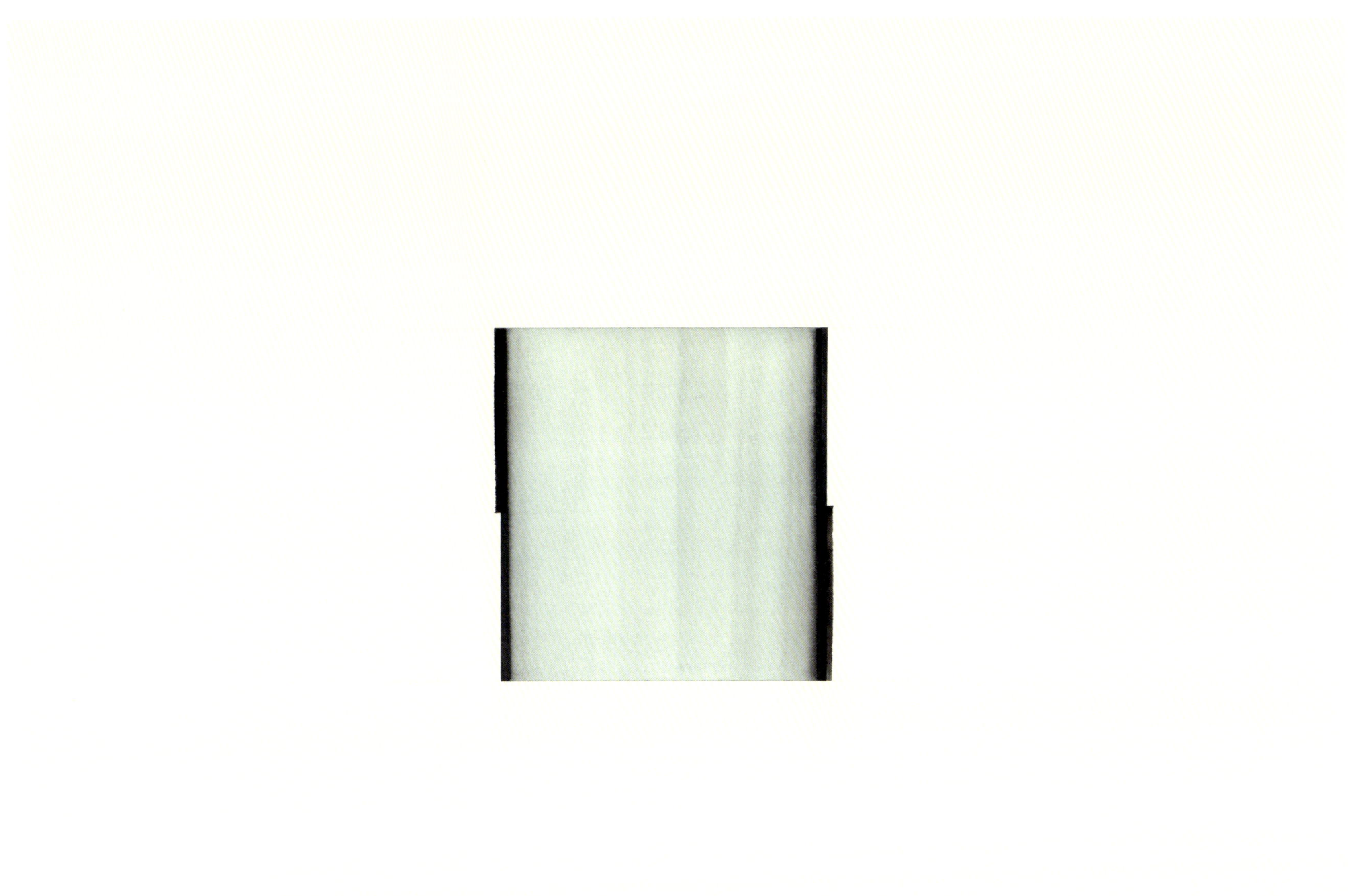

callum innes was born in edinburgh in 1962, he studied drawing and painting at gray's school of art from 1980 to 1984 and then completed a postgraduate degree at edinburgh college of art, in 1985.

he began exhibiting in the mid-to-late 1980s and in 1992 had two major exhibitions in public galleries, at the ica, london, and the scottish national gallery of modern art, edinburgh. since then he has emerged as one of the most significant abstract painters of his generation, achieving widespread recognition through major solo and group shows worldwide.

innes was shortlisted for the turner and jerwood prizes in 1995, won the prestigious natwest prize for painting in 1998, and in 2002 was awarded the jerwood prize for painting. he has exhibited widely both nationally and internationally and his work is held in public collections worldwide including the guggenheim, new york; centre pompidou, paris; fort worth museum, texas; tate, london, and scottish national gallery of modern art.

recent major solo exhibitions include *in position* at chateau la coste, 2019, france; and in 2016 the exhibition *i'll close my eyes*, at de pont museum, tilburg. the accompanying monograph of the same title, published by hatje cantz, offered a broad survey of innes' practice, exhibiting works on canvas, oilpaper, watercolours and painting directly onto the wall surface, from the late 1980s until the present. previously the major solo exhibition, *from memory*, was shown at the fruitmarket gallery, edinburgh in 2007, touring to modern art oxford, and the museum of contemporary art, sydney.

the poet thomas a clark lives in a fishing village on the east coast of scotland. his selected poems, *the threadbare coat*, was published by carcanet press in 2020. during the summer months, with the artist laurie clark, he runs cairn gallery, a space for minimal and conceptual art.

the exhibition *a pure land* is a collaboration between
osl contemporary, oslo and i8 gallery, reykjavik, 2021

all watercolours
2020
on arches 600gsm hp
76.5 × 57.5 cm

the artist would like to thank

kristin nordhøy

thomas a clark, laurie clark

emilie magnus, borkur arnarson

david jenkins, petter snare

herman lelie and stefania bonelli

ewan mcclure, alun scurlock, thomas whittle, joanna chia-yu lin

jane hamlyn, sean kelly and darragh hogan

first published in 2021 by circa press

circa press
50 great portland street
london w1w 7nd
www.circa.press

isbn 978-1-911422-15-0

design and production: herman lelie
layout: stefania bonelli
photography: øystein thorvaldsen
reproduction: dexter premedia
printed and bound by ebs, italy